Factoid: Deserts get fewer than 10 inches of rain a year.

MathStart®
ROUNDING

Coyotes
All Around

by Stuart J. Murphy • illustrated by Steve Björkman

HarperCollins Publishers

LEVEL
2

To Duncan and Alia—
Who are as clever as coyotes
—S.J.M.

For Sage and Sierra,
who know coyotes
—S.B.

The publisher and author would like to thank teachers Patricia Chase, Phyllis Goldman,
and Patrick Hopfensperger for their help in making the math in
MathStart just right for kids.

HarperCollins®, 🛋®, and MathStart® are registered trademarks of HarperCollins Publishers.
For more information about the MathStart series, write to HarperCollins Children's Books,
1350 Avenue of the Americas, New York, NY 10019, or visit our website at
www.mathstartbooks.com.

Bugs incorporated in the MathStart series design were painted by Jon Buller.

Coyotes All Around
Text copyright © 2003 by Stuart J. Murphy
Illustrations copyright © 2003 by Steve Björkman
Manufactured in Hong Kong. All rights reserved.

Library of Congress Cataloging-in-Publication Data
Murphy, Stuart J., 1942–
Coyotes all around / by Stuart J. Murphy ; illustrated by Steve Björkman.— 1st ed.
p.   cm. — (MathStart)
"Level 2, rounding."
Summary: A pack of coyotes tries to determine how many roadrunners and other creatures
are in their vicinity, and while some count different groups and add their totals together,
Clever Coyote rounds off and estimates.
ISBN 0-06-051529-5 — ISBN 0-06-051531-7 (pbk.)
1. Estimation theory—Juvenile literature.   2. Coyote—Juvenile literature.
3. Roadrunner—Juvenile literature.   [1. Estimations theory.   2. Counting.
3. Coyote.   4. Desert animals.]   I. Björkman, Steve, ill.   II. Title.   III. Series.
QA276 .M88   2003   2002151776
519 .5'44—dc21

Typography by Elynn Cohen   6 7 8 9 10   ❖   First Edition

Coyotes All Around

One afternoon, a pack of coyotes gathered on the porch of their desert ranch.

"Look at all those roadrunners," said Clumsy Coyote.

"Mmmm," said Clever Coyote. "Isn't it just about lunchtime?"

"There must be hundreds of them!" said Cool Coyote.

4

"Hundreds!" said Clever Coyote. "That's ridiculous. There can't be that many. Why don't you guys count and see how many there really are?"

Factoid: *Coyote* can be pronounced "KY-oht" or "ky-OH-tee."

5

Clumsy Coyote said, "I'll take this side."
Careful Coyote took the smallest coyote, Little One, and said, "Let's try over here."

"I've got the best side," bragged Cool Coyote.
Everyone started counting.
Everyone except Clever Coyote.

Factoid: Roadrunners can fly, but they usually run. They can go as fast as 15 miles an hour.

7

Clever Coyote was starting to get hungry. While everybody was busy counting, she slunk. She crept. She jumped! She missed.

Factoid: Coyotes will eat almost anything—from rabbits and mice to insects, berries, fruit, and even garbage.

9

"Oof!" said Clever Coyote. "That ground was hard. So how many birds were there?"

"I need a piece of paper to add everything up," said Careful.

"Ha!" said Clever Coyote. "I bet I can do it in my head and come really close."

"No way," said Little One.

Factoid: Coyotes can be found all over North America.

0 1 2 3 4 5 6 7 8 9 10 11 12 13 14 15 16 17 18 19 20 21 22 23 24 25 26 27 28 29 30

21 is very close to 20.

12 is close to 10.

17 is closer to 20 than to 10.

And 8 is almost 10.

Adding tens is easy!

$$\begin{array}{r} 20 \\ 10 \\ 20 \\ + \ 10 \\ \hline 60 \end{array}$$

"Around 60 roadrunners," said Clever Coyote.
Careful took out a pencil and paper and added up the numbers.
"It's exactly 58," he said. "She was just a little over."
"They don't call me Clever for nothing," said Clever Coyote.

$$
\begin{array}{r}
2^1 \\
12 \\
17 \\
+\ 8 \\
\hline
58
\end{array}
$$

"I bet there are lots of lizards out there," said Clumsy. "Where there are roadrunners, there are lizards."

"Hey, you're right," said Cool Coyote. "It looks like there are thousands of them!"

"There can't be that many," said Clever Coyote. "Why don't you count them and see?"

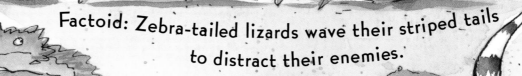

Factoid: Zebra-tailed lizards wave their striped tails to distract their enemies.

16

Clever Coyote was very hungry.
While everybody was busy counting, she prowled.
She stalked. She pounced!
She missed.

Factoid: Most adult coyotes are about 4 feet long (from tip to tail) and 2 feet tall.

17

"Ouch," said Clever Coyote. "That rock was really pointy. So how many lizards were there?"

"I'll get my paper," said Careful.

"Don't bother," said Clever Coyote. "I'll do it in my head again."

11 is just 1 over 10.

13 is closer to 10 than to 20.

27 is closer to 30 than to 20.

2 is a lot closer to 0 than to 10.

Now I'll add up all my tens.

$$
\begin{array}{r}
10 \\
10 \\
30 \\
+\ 0 \\
\hline
50
\end{array}
$$

"Around 50 lizards,"
Clever Coyote said.

Careful wrote the numbers down and added them up.
"It's exactly 53," he said. "She was just a little under."
"That's why they call me Clever," said Clever Coyote.

$$\begin{array}{r} 11 \\ 13 \\ 27 \\ +\ 2 \\ \hline 53 \end{array}$$

"There must be a lot of grasshoppers," said Clumsy. "Where there are lizards, there are always grasshoppers."

"Look, you're right," said Cool Coyote. "There could be a million of them!"

Factoid: Coyotes live alone, in pairs, or in groups.

"Oh, stop exaggerating," said Clever Coyote. "Go ahead and count them up."

23

Clever Coyote was starving. While everybody was busy counting, she lurked. She hid. She leaped! She missed.

Factoid: Grasshoppers can jump distances up to 200 times their body length.

"Yow!" said Clever Coyote. "That was a really prickly cactus!
So how many grasshoppers were there?"
"Where's my paper?" asked Careful.

"Never mind," said Clever Coyote. "I bet I can come really close again. But if I do, you guys have to gather some beetles for lunch. They're my favorite!"

"You're on," said Clumsy. "You'll never do it 3 times in a row."

Factoid: A saguaro cactus can grow as tall as 50 feet and live as many as 200 years.

0 1 2 3 4 5 6 7 8 9 10 11 (12) 13 14 15 16 17 (18) 19 20 21 22 23 (24) (25) 26 27 28 29 30

24 is closer to 20 than to 30.

18 is almost 20.

25 is halfway between 20 and 30. I'll go up to 30.

12 is closer to 10 than to 20.

Now I'll add up all my tens.

"Around 80 grasshoppers,"
Clever Coyote said.

$$
\begin{array}{r}
20 \\
20 \\
30 \\
+\ 10 \\
\hline
80
\end{array}
$$

Careful wrote the numbers down and added them up. "By gosh! She did it," he shouted. "The exact answer is 79," he said. "She was *really* close this time."

"Clever Coyote does it again," said Clever. "Now hurry up with those beetles." She smacked her lips.

$$\begin{array}{r} 24 \\ 18 \\ 25 \\ +\ 12 \\ \hline 79 \end{array}$$

Clumsy jumped. Careful pounced. Cool leaped. And Little One followed. They landed right on top of Clever Coyote.

"I guess it's about time I gave up on lunch," groaned not-so-Clever Coyote from the bottom of the pile.

31

In *Coyotes All Around*, the math concept is rounding. Rounding is one way to estimate the sum of several numbers. Knowledge of place value is key to the child's understanding of rounding and estimating whole numbers.

If you would like to have more fun with the math concepts presented in *Coyotes All Around*, here are a few suggestions:

Note: If the number in the ones column is 4 or less, then round down to the nearest ten (42 becomes 40). If the number in the ones column is 5 or greater, then round up to the nearest ten (47 becomes 50).

• Reread the story and point out how Clever Coyote uses the number line to round each of the numbers.

• Talk with the child about why it is easier to add numbers after they have been rounded to the nearest ten.

• Make up an addition problem consisting of three 2-digit numbers [for example, 14+37+23] and have the child round each number [10+40+20] and find the sum. Have the child use a calculator to find the sum of the unrounded numbers and compare this answer to his or her estimate.

• Take the face cards out of a deck of cards and place the deck face down between two or more players. Each player takes a turn drawing 2 cards and uses them to make a double-digit number (for example, a 5 and a 2 would be 52). The players round their numbers (52 would round to 50) and the player with the highest number wins.

When rounding 1- or 2- digit numbers to the nearest 10, numbers that end in 4 or lower should be rounded **down.**

So a 42 becomes a 40.

Following are some activities that will help you extend the concepts presented in *Coyotes All Around* into a child's everyday life:

Three in a Row: Take 9 blank index cards and write the following numbers on them: 17, 24, 1, 12, 8, 31, 29, 36, and 4. Place these cards face down into the "pool." On a sheet of paper, create a grid as displayed below. The first player picks 3 numbers from the pool. The player rounds each chosen number and finds the sum of the rounded numbers. He or she places a marker (buttons, coins, or small colored pieces of paper will work) over the sum in the grid. The first player to have three markers in a row is the winner.

GRID:

70	60	30	40
50	10	10	80
100	80	40	20
30	50	70	60

Grocery Shopping: Have the child estimate the number of cereal boxes on each shelf. Then have the child count all the boxes and compare the total to their estimate.

The following books include some of the same concepts that are presented in *Coyotes All Around*:

- MATH FOR ALL SEASONS by Greg Tang
- COUNTING CROCODILES by Judy Sierra
- COUNTING ON FRANK by Rod Clement
- MOIRA'S BIRTHDAY by Robert N. Munsch

Numbers that end in 5 or higher should be rounded **up**.

That means a 47 becomes a 50.